KEY WEST

BY GERALD SPRAYREGEN

DEDICATION TO:
Frances (Gordon) Sprayregen   1907–1996
Herman Sprayregen   1898–1980

Parents of: Carol, Gerald, and Seymour   Grandparents of: David, Nicholas, Lisa, Pamela, and Sharon

Great Grandparents of: Nicole, Matthew, Melanie, Emily, Jesse, Jonathan, Benjamin, Nicole, and Alexa

1934

*A day never passes when I do not reflect on my mother's smile, beauty, sense of humor and gentleness,
my father's wisdom and strength, and the love I received from both of them. GS*

ACKNOWLEDGMENT

My sincere thanks to the following individuals and organizations for their help, advice and suggestions in helping me create *Key West*: Bob Cardenas, Tom McCarrain, Sam Trophia, Mark Prokopeak, Kelly Tavares, Buck Banks, Norman Aberele, Norman Woods, Sr., Betty Sammis, Nancy Forester, Joe Allen, Paul Collins, Jacque Sands, Dan Burley, Peter Green, Donna Edward, Carol Wrightman, Gharavi Mohammad, Sharon Wells, Winifred Shine Fryzel, Renee Onorato, John Brancati, John Miller, Paul Hause, Gerard Nudo, and R.R. Donnelley.

My grateful appreciation and special thanks to the following for their suggestions and information, which have all been incorporated into *Key West*: Mel Cowher, Tom Tong, Wendy Xu, Heather Peres, and Dr. Seymour Sprayregen.

I am forever indebted to Gloria Sophia who spent many months working on this project with me while simultaneously devoting hundreds of hours to typing the various drafts of the manuscript for Key West.

BIBLIOGRAPHY

Papa – Hemingway in Key West
– James McLendon
Langley Press, Inc.- 1972 revised -1990

Key West Houses – Leslie Linsley
Rizzoli N.Y. - 1992

Key West – History of an Island of Dreams
– Maureen Ogle
University Press of Florida - 2003

The Houses of Key West – Alex Caemmerer
Pineapple Press, Sarasota, Fl. - 1992

Walking and Biking Guide
 – to Historic Key West – Sharon Wells,
Sharon Wells Company, Key West, Fl.- 2003

Key West Gardens and Their Stories
 – Janis Frawley-Holler,
Pineapple Press, Sarasota, Fl. – 2000

Shell's Key West Classics and Challenge –
2003

Key Wester – Katharine Roach
Gorden B. Brown, Jr. – April 2003

First printing - December 2003
Second printing - May 2004
Published by
Gerald Sprayregen Productions
10 Southeastern Farms Road
Pound Ridge, New York 10576
914-234-2618

Printed and bound by R.R. Donnelley – China
ISBN: 0-9746299-0-1
Library of Congress Catalog
Card Number: 2003097592

TABLE OF CONTENTS

THE GRAND DAMES OF KEY WEST

GARDENS OF KEY WEST

Key West, with its fascinating 28,000 citizens, is a tropical paradise, squeezed between the Gulf of Mexico and the Atlantic Ocean, at the southernmost tip of the United States. Key West is only 90 miles from Cuba and 150 miles from Miami. The island itself, roughly two by four miles, is partially surrounded by live coral reefs, which are so unique they attract people from all over the world.

Key West has a intriguing history, because of its inhabitants, its climate, and its hype. It keeps reinventing itself, much to the displeasure of the conchs, a nickname given to anything original to Key West.

Key West has a long and colorful past, beginning with its European discovery in 1815 by Ponce de Leon. The island was originally known as Cayo Hueso (Isle of Bones) because it was littered with remains from an Indian battlefield. Unfortunately, the majority of archeological artifacts have been lost or destroyed by time. The name Key West is the English translation of the Spanish name.

In 1821, John Simonton purchased Key West for $2,000 from Jean Pablo Solas. Solas had received the property in 1815 from the Spanish Government for favors he had performed years earlier.

In 1821, Andrew Jackson led a group of Americans to Pensacola, Florida to witness the transfer of Florida from the Spanish government to the United States. A short time later, a naval base was established there, to try to stop pirates. Since 1821, the presence of the US Navy has been a major factor in the growth and development of Key West, which was incorporated in 1828.

In the 1800s, pirates ruled the seas around Florida, stopping any ships they could find, taking their valuable cargo, and often killing all passengers and crewmembers. Because of this, the owners of merchant vessels demanded action. Congress responded in 1822 by ordering that all pirates be eradicated in the Florida area. Commander David Porter was put in charge of a squad of ships and 1,100 men. Porter turned the tables on the pirates, burning their ships and killing the pirates who did not flee the area. In less than two years, all pirates were eliminated. It is estimated that there were 100 people in Key West in 1823, and by 1830 this increased to over 500, brave, hearty souls. During these early years, Key West was branded as a place for drinkers, killers, and in general, an unsavory place. This reputation only seemed to increase the interest of many Americans, who are basically imbued with a pioneering spirit.

During the early 19th century, all ships carrying cargo between Cuba and the United States had to attempt to outmaneuver the dangerous reef-filled waters, which held Key West captive. This particular set of circumstances created a utopia for the New England seamen, who along with the Bahamians, created Key West's first major industry, that of salvaging cargo from the treacherous coral reefs. Many of the early homes of Key West were built and furnished utilizing the spoils of these shipwrecks. For approximately 25 years the salvage industry flourished, but as lighthouses became more common, the salvage business lost its profitability.

The sponge industry began in the 1840s, and is the only major industry started in the 19th century in Key West which has continued to survive and prosper. Fortunately for the Key West sponge industry, there are a number of fields such as the medical field, which need fibers of natural sponges.

Sunset Key

In the late 1800s, many Cubans were leaving Cuba because of the Spanish-Cuban territorial wars. Since Key West was only 90 miles away, it attracted the Cubans, who arrived with their cigar-making experience. The first cigar factory was opened in 1831, and by 1890 there were over 150 separate cigar factories in Key West. The cigar industry created thousands of jobs for the 17,000 residents of Key West. In the early 1900s, because of labor unrest, many cigar makers moved to Tampa, Florida. In 1880, Key West had the distinction of having more inhabitants than any other city in Florida, and was also the richest city per capita in the United States. In 1890, the population of Florida was 700,000 people.

In 1905, Henry Flagler, co-founder with John D. Rockefeller of Standard Oil, announced plans to build a railroad from Miami to Key West, which would link Key West to the rest of Florida. At that time, everyone and everything entering Key West came by ship because at that point there were neither roads nor rail into Key West. Flagler was the developer of Palm Beach, but this monumental undertaking was considered by many as Flagler's folly. There were over 40 bridges that had to be built, and one was seven miles long. The residents of Key West viewed these incredible plans with delight, and felt if that enormous undertaking were successful, it would make Key West more desirable than Miami or Palm Beach. The railroad from Miami to Key West was completed in seven years, covering over 140 miles of swampy wilderness and open seas, and cost over $125 million dollars. Over 200 men lost their lives during the construction of this monumental undertaking, due to hurricanes and other tragedies. Flagler died one year after its completion.

During the Great Depression in 1932, with the exception of "Papa" Hemmingway, and a few others, virtually every citizen in Key West was on relief. Key West was totally bankrupt and turned its charter back to the state and federal governments. President Roosevelt hired Julius Stone to save the city. Mr. Stone created a new tourist campaign which advertised Key West as "America's Bermuda." Millions of dollars were poured in by the Florida Emergency Relief Administration Fund. Attractions for Key West had to be built, and the first project was the first open-air aquarium in the country.

During the Second World War, Key West was the base of operations supporting naval destroyers and aircraft. In 1940, it became a training base. Shortly thereafter, President Harry S. Truman established his vacation home, "The Little White House" in Key West. Population more than doubled from 1940 to 1960, and tourism increased substantially. In 1960, there were approximately 50,000 people living in Key West, which included 20,000 military with their families and two to four thousand civilian employees. During the next 20 years the population decreased by 25%, due mainly to a cutback in naval personnel. Once again, the city re-emphasized tourism, as it did in the forties, and tourism became its major industry. During this time, Duval Street and Old Town were refurbished. Businesses were started and Key West, once again, became a popular place to visit. Many old homes were renovated, mostly by the gay population, and the value of property increased substantially. Today, Key West is an international destination, and home to more published authors per square mile than any other spot in America.

HOUSE BOATS
1801 North Roosevelt Boulevard

During the 1950s a number of houseboat owners sailed their vessels into Key West, found it to their liking, and tied up along South Roosevelt Boulevard at the Atlantic Ocean. Word spread, more houseboats arrived, and over the next number of years houseboats became a common sight on the Atlantic side of Key West. Since the houseboat owners were enjoying "squatters rights" (no rent), they decided to go one step further and plugged into the city's electrical system. Certainly from their point of view, free electricity was included in their squatters rights' package. The city of Key West felt a little differently, which is the cloth from which lawsuits are made. The city went to court to get rid of the squatters. The squatters liked "Paradise" and wanted to stay. The court battle went on for five decades. The squatters got older, some died and some new ones came, but the fight continued. Strangely enough, nature became the magistrate, and in 1998 hurricane George, while wreaking havoc on Key West, destroyed virtually all but a few of the houseboats. To add insult to injury for the poor squatters, the city finally got a court order forcing them to vacate. A few relocated to Garrison Bight, part of the city marina; some chose to seek their future elsewhere. Today there are approximately 88 "live-aboards" at Garrison Bight.

11

THE SHOT GUN HOUSE
411 Truman Avenue

During the late 19th Century "The Shot Gun House" became the prevailing home to be built in Key West. As cigar making rose to become the leading industry in Key West, it employed more than 5,000 individuals, which represented more than 16% of the population of the city. A need to build small inexpensive homes for the workers of the cigar factories arose. The Shot Gun House solved the problem perfectly. Originally conceived and built in West Africa, these homes were clustered together on a track of land and built quickly. These single-story, one-room wide buildings, were usually a set of three rooms, one behind the other, where, if a bullet were shot from the front doorway, it could pass through the house, out the back door, without touching a wall. There are numerous variations of this style, some quite sophisticated in design. These homes are constantly being restored and are quite desirable in Key West today.

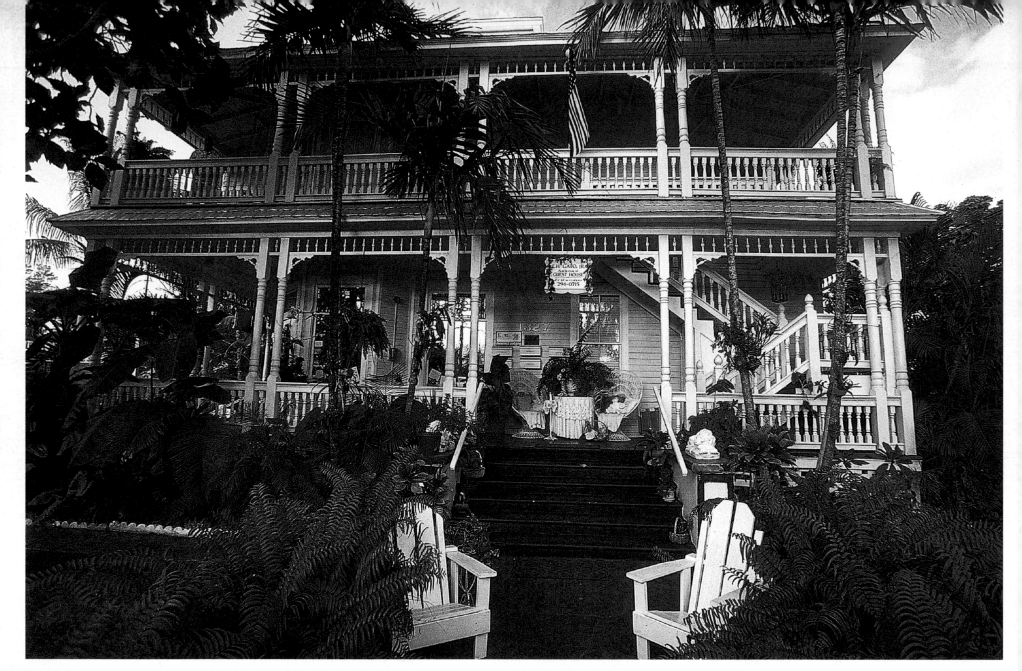

E. H. GATO JR. HOUSE

1327 Duval Street

This beautiful example of Victorian architecture (circa 1885), was built by Edward Hidalgo Gato for his son. The elder Gato left Cuba in the 1860s and became a legend in the Key West cigar industry.

Originally, this house was across the street facing South, but Mr. Gato was uncomfortable with the noonday heat on the porch, and so with the help of an army of mules, moved the house across the street. Interestingly enough, the street number 1327 never changed, and today it is the only odd-numbered house on that side of Duval Street. The house remained in the Gato family until the 1930s when it was sold. Today the E.H. Gato Jr. House is the southernmost guesthouse in the United States and is a very charming place to stay.

CATS

Make no mistake about it . . . Cats rule this Island! They go any place they want, sleep anywhere they find comfortable, gobble food indiscriminately off any table, and never, never get reprimanded. In the Hemingway Estate, there is a cat burial ground for approximately 60 cats, all previous inhabitants of 907 Whitehead Street. The cats were named after celebrities such as Spencer Tracy, Elizabeth Taylor and Shakespeare; currently the oldest living cat is Marilyn Monroe, age 19. Interestingly enough, at least half of the Hemingway cats are polydactyl (more than five toes).

Charlette is seated on this page and on the opposite page is Anna.

BICYCLES

The conch mode of transportation in Key West is the bicycle. No self-respecting resident would drive or walk to an island location if it could be reached by bicycle.

CARS

People who live in Key West year round are different. . . It is not 100% necessary to be a little eccentric, but if you are unconventional, odd, strange, bizarre, idiosyncratic, peculiar, whimsical, quirky, cranky, screwy, nonconformist, crackpot, oddball, weirdo, or a screwball, it would help.

KEY WEST SECESSION

If there is a single "high water mark" in the history of Key West, it is April 23, 1982. All Conchs point to that milestone day with pride because on that day Key West and the Florida Keys seceded from the U.S. and became the Conch Republic. A little history will explain this plan.

On April 18th, 1982, the U.S. Border Patrol set up a roadblock on U.S.I in Florida City to search all vehicles coming from Key West. This surprise barricade was set up on a Sunday afternoon as hundreds of visitors were leaving the Keys on the one and only road to Miami and the rest of the world. A 19 mile traffic jam developed, which prompted hundreds of calls to Key West Mayor Dennis Wardlow. Wardlow realized that if this roadblock continued, tourism would be incredibly diminished. The Border Patrol stated "We're checking on illegal aliens coming into the Keys," and later admitted, "drug interdiction" was the second motive. The Mayor and a group of delegates filed a federal injunction to force the Border Patrol to remove the roadblock. Unfortunately, the injunction was denied. On the way back from court in Miami, David Horan, the Key West attorney, while flying the delegates home to Key West, decided to aggressively buzz the roadblock and the Border Patrol. He was rewarded for his heroism by being named Secretary of the Conch Republic Air Force a few days later. On Friday, April 23rd, the day following the court's decision, the Conch Republic was born; its birthplace, Mallory Dock. Mayor Wardlow became Prime Minister, and ambassadors were appointed to Hawaii, Texas, and other important geographical locations.

Immediately, the new republic declared war on the United States, and its ships fired shots of conch fritters and old Cuban bread at navy personnel. Fortunately no one was injured, and within moments the new republic surrendered and requested millions of dollars in federal aid.

Thanks to the public relations work done by Stuart Newman, of Stuart Newman Associates, the entire episode received substantial media attention throughout the country. Each year the Key West declaration of independence is commemorated with a mock air and sea battle, with airplanes bombing with toilet paper, and ships shooting red dye and old Cuban bread.

KEY WEST TREASURE CHEST   700 Front Street

O n July 20, 1985, Mel Fisher, who is now acknowledged to be the world's greatest treasure hunter, received a marine radio transmission from his son, Kane, who was captain of one of the salvage vessels that had been searching for the Spanish galleon Atocha. Kanes's message was simple: "Put away the charts. We found the mother lode." Mel's life-long dream was about to be realized, because the "mother lode" in this case represented approximately $400,000,000 worth of gold, silver, emeralds and artifacts. After lying on the ocean floor for more than 360 years unmolested, the Atocha was finally giving up her riches. Thousands of gold and silver coins and bars, beautifully handcrafted gold link chains (some more than 50 feet in length), thousands of emeralds, and countless, priceless artifacts, including cannons, weapons, personal jewelry, ornate gold plates and goblets, and various types of pottery comprised the bounty. For 17 years, Mel's motto had been "Today's the day." July 20, 1985 actually became that day. Ironically, the discovery of this fortune came exactly ten years to the day after Mel and his devoted wife, Dolores, lost their son Dirk and daughter-in-law, Angel, when their salvage vessel, Northwind, took on water in the middle of the night and capsized, trapping the young couple and another diver, Rick Gage, inside the vessel.

In September of 1622, the Nuestra Senora de Atocha, along with 27 other ships of King Philip IV's Tierra Firme Fleet, left Havana, Cuba with Spain as their destination. Unfortunately, the vessels were caught in a severe hurricane, and eight ships, including the Atocha and the Santa Margarita, were destroyed by the treacherous reefs off the Florida Keys. The Atocha, as the flagship of the fleet, carried the most prominent passengers and widest assortment of treasures. Of its 265 passengers, only five individuals lived to tell the story.

In 1963, Mel had a fortuitous meeting with a Florida treasure hunter, Kip Wagner, who, along with his associates had been attempting to salvage the remains of the Spanish Fleet lost on the East Coast of Florida in 1715. Mel and Kip then became equal partners in their ventures. Although the 1715 Spanish shipwrecks were close to shore, and the divers were sometimes working in only ten feet of water, the water was extremely murky, and often visibility was zero. Fortunately, with Mel's engineering background he created a device he called a "mailbox" which, when lowered from the vessel would send a layer of clear water downward so that the divers could clearly see where they were working. The "mailbox" also was able to part the sand so that the divers could uncover the buried treasures. Over the next six years, the partners uncovered more than $20 million worth of treasures from the 1715 shipwrecks.

In 1968, Mel and his fledgling company, Treasure Salvors, Inc., began their search for one of the richest shipwrecks in history, the Nuestra Senora de Atocha. Over the next 17 years, Mel committed himself and his family to the quest of finding the Atocha, and he overcame personal, legal and financial trials that would have stopped anyone, except Mel Fisher.

In 1974, Mel sought the legal services of David Paul Horan. Over the next decade, Horan successfully litigated and defended Mel's companies, Treasure Salvors, Inc., and Cobb Coin Company, from claims of the United States of America, the State of Florida and numerous other opportunists. In 1982, Horan argued Fisher's case before the United States Supreme Court. In a 5 to 4 decision, the highest court in the land ruled that Treasure Salvors was the sole owner of everything recovered from the Nuestra Senora de Atocha. David Paul Horan, had become the world's foremost authority on the salvage of shipwrecks. Horan and his brother and law partner, Edward W. Horan, have been primary counsel for such notable shipwrecks as the RMS Titanic (lost in the North Atlantic in 1912), the SS Central America (lost off the East Coast of North America in 1857), the San Miguel de Archangel (lost off Florida's East Coast in 1659) and El Cazador (lost off Louisiana in 1784).

Judge William O. Mehrtens of the United States District Court of the Southern District of Florida summed up Mel's situation in his August 21, 1978 ruling against the State of Florida, when he stated: "The finding of a great treasure from the days of the Spanish Main is not the cherished dream of only the United States and Florida citizens; countless people from other lands have shared such thoughts. It would amaze and surprise most citizens of this country, when their dream, at the greatest of costs, was realized, that agents of respective governments would, on the most flimsy grounds, lay claim to the treasure."

The beautiful, exciting and authentic treasures of Key West Treasure Chest are, in part, the legal fees David Paul and Edward Horan received for their successful efforts regarding the Atocha, lost off the Florida Keys in 1622.

Photo of diver taken by Don Kincaid

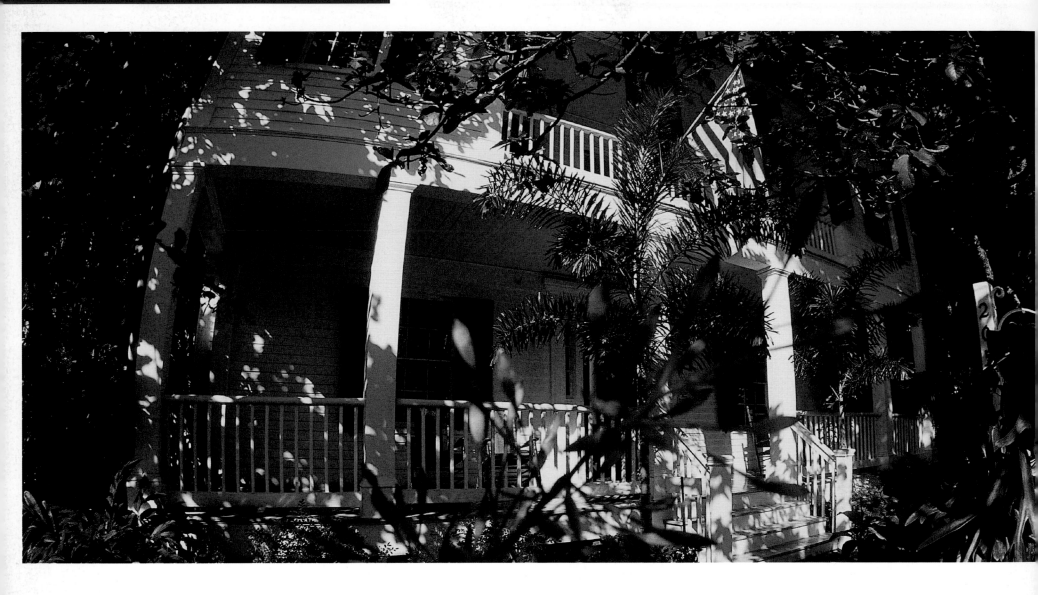

AUDUBON HOUSE AND TROPICAL GARDENS
205 Whitehead Street

In the mid 1800s, Captain John Geiger, a wealthy wrecker, started to create this unique setting. John J. Audubon, the world-renowned naturalist, spent many days and nights as a guest of the captain and painted many of his celebrated birds of America in these surroundings. In 1960, Mitchell Wolfson, of Wometco fame, completed the restoration of this unique house and gardens. This oasis of lush plants and trees from around the world, coupled with dazzling displays of beautifully-colored flowers creates a respite of gentleness in Key West. Perhaps this is why so many brides and grooms choose this spot to pledge their love.

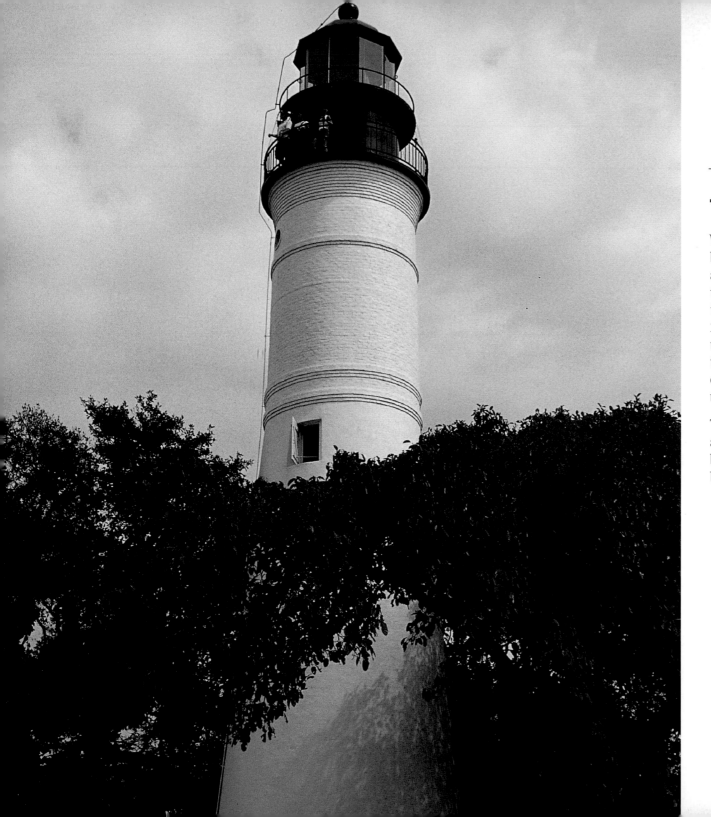

KEY WEST
LIGHTHOUSE MUSEUM
938 Whitehead Street

The Key West Lighthouse was built in 1847. It replaced the original wooden tower on Whitehead Point, which was destroyed in the hurricane of 1846. The present location, 14 feet above sea level, was chosen to protect the new tower from a similar fate. This brick tower is 86 feet high; 88 steps inside lead to a balcony with a 360-degree view of Key West. This is one of the most attractive vantage points in Key West to view the entire island. In 1969, the U.S. Coastal Board decommissioned the Lighthouse. In 1989, it was restored as a historical site at a cost of $265,000.

The lighthouse keeper's quarters was built in 1887, and today houses the museum's collection of lighthouse artifacts and the maritime history of Key West.

PRESIDENTIAL GATES
Whitehead Street corner of Caroline

President Truman made these gates famous when he visited Key West. Each morning he began his five-mile constitutional walk through these gates, with secret service agents in tow. These beautiful gates were built in 1906, and until 1987 would only be opened for visiting dignitaries.

THE HARRY S. TRUMAN LITTLE WHITE HOUSE MUSEUM
111 Front Street

The Harry S. Truman Little White House Museum is a 8,700 square foot, two-story Victorian building which was constructed in 1890 at a cost of $7,000. In 1991 it was restored and opened as a museum at a cost of one million dollars. It was originally built as housing for the naval station commander. Thomas Edison lived here while donating his services to the U.S. World I effort in 1917.

This site has a history that dates back to 1823, when the U.S. Government eradicated the pirates of the area. It was also a strategic port for the Spanish-American War, a submarine base for World War II, and a much-discussed position during the Cuban Missile Crisis in 1962. Harry S. Truman, the 33rd President of the United States, first visited Key West in 1946. He liked the climate and enjoyed taking his five-mile morning constitutional walk. President Truman loved the fishing, and returned ten more times for a total of 175 days during his presidency, which lasted from 1945 to 1952.

After Truman paved the way, a number of other presidents utilized the attractive facilities of the Little White House. In 1955, President Eisenhower while recovering from a heart attack, held all his meetings in this house. In 1961, President Kennedy held a summit meeting here with Britain's Prime Minister three weeks before the Bay of Pigs Invasion, and just prior to the Vietnam buildup. A year later, immediately after the Cuban Missile Crisis, President Kennedy paid Key West another visit to assure the people of the United States it was safe to visit Florida.

29

THE CUSTOM HOUSE
AND
KEY WEST MUSEUM OF ART AND HISTORY
281 Front Street

This imposing 1891 magnificently designed redbrick building built in 1891, is a registered national landmark, and one of the most beautiful and important buildings in Key West. It cost approximately $110,000 to build. In 1999 a major restoration, which took nine years, was completed at a cost of nine million dollars. It originally served as a Federal Building, housing the Post Office and Custom Service. On the second floor was the Federal District Court, in which the original hearing was held to determine the cause of the sinking of the U.S.S. Maine in Havana in 1898.

Today the building serves as the Key West Museum of Art and History. There are ten to twelve exhibitions each year in addition to the permanent exhibits. "Who Is Key West" is a portrait collection of Key West notables and nefarious characters by nationally renowned artist Paul Collins. Because of its popularity, this exhibition is on extended loan from the artist.

This building is one of three historic buildings operated as museums by the Key West Art and Historical Society. The Key West Lighthouse and East Martello Tower (a Civil War Fort) are also operated by the society.

THE KEY WEST HISTORIC MEMORIAL GARDEN
Mallory Dock

The most compelling work of art in Key West today is "The Wreckers," the centerpiece of The Key West Historic Memorial Garden. This depicts two wreckers on a sinking ship with a little girl strapped to the back of one of the men. Her left arm is clinging to the neck of her savior and her right arm is holding her doll. Surrounding this emotional bronze is a series of 36 busts of the men and women who were important to the development of Key West, from 1821 until 1980. James Mastin, an award-winning sculptor from Miami, created "The Wreckers." Simonton, who purchased Key West in 1821, Flagler, who built the railroad, and Hemingway are all honored with their images cast in bronze, with plaques describing their importance to Key West.

This garden was created in September 1997 as a memorial to those courageous men and women who helped create the Key West we know today.

THE WRECKERS

KEY WEST CEMETERY
Center of Old Town
Bounded by Angela, Margaret, Passover Lane , Frances, and Olivia

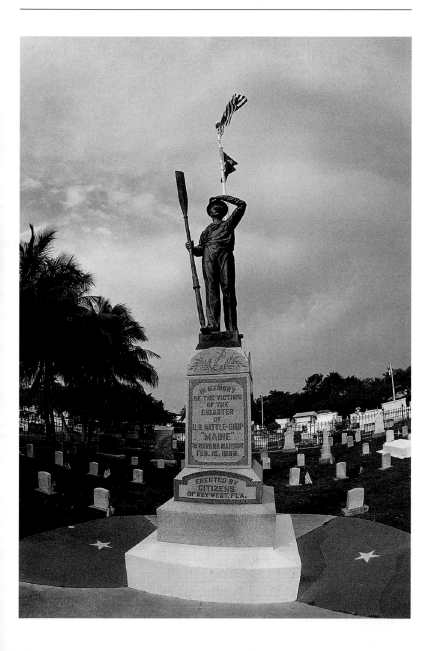

Where else in the world can one find a cemetery located in the heart of town, and spend an enjoyable half day reading tombstones, and chuckling or laughing out loud? In 1847 a severe hurricane washed away the entire graveyard and the dead were scattered throughout the forest, many of them lodged in the branches of nearby trees.

After that disaster, the cemetery was relocated to higher ground. Because of the rocky foundation of the island, all tombs are above ground. The largest and most visible gravesite is that of 27 sailors of the U.S.S. Maine, destroyed in Havana, Cuba in 1898. Although there was no concrete proof of responsibility for the act, the combination of the press and the outcry from the public forced the U.S. Government to declare war on Spain. Pictured below is a conch (born in Key West) woman who married in Key West, raised a family here, and now visits her husband who died a few years ago. She recently moved north, but whenever she returns, she visits her husband's grave site and enjoys a breakfast of a croissant and a cup of coffee.

On Violet Street you will find the grave of Joe Russell, proprietor of Sloppy Joe's, and a buddy and constant companion of Hemingway's. Russel died while deep-sea fishing with "Papa" in 1941. A number of blocks away, you will see the markings for Thomas Romer, a black Bohemian, with the inscription, "Good Citizen for 65 of his 108 years," signed by Gallagher, perhaps an opinionated stonecutter. Another grave has the inscription, "Devoted fan of Julio Iglesias." My favorite is the inscription on a crypt in the Jewish section of the cemetery that reads, "I told you I was sick." There is also an interesting comment, probably by a former wife, "At least I know where he is sleeping tonight."

KEY WEST AQUARIUM
1 Whitehead Street

In 1932, during the Great Depression, Key West was bankrupt. The Florida Emergency Relief Administration Fund was initiated by President Franklin Roosevelt to save the city. The Key West Aquarium was its first project, and was constructed from 1932 to 1934.

From the beginning, getting really close to the fish and animals has always been a unique part of the Aquarium's experience. The touch tank, which permits children and grown-ups to hold and touch the fish and animals, has always been a major attraction. The aquarium was renovated in 1983 and is now primarily enclosed. It has numerous tanks which house a large and beautiful collection of fish indigenous to the Keys. Shark feedings (eight times a day) have been thrilling crowds for decades.

KEY WEST BUTTERFLY AND NATURE CONSERVATORY

1316 Duval Street

Perhaps the most eye-catching and beautiful attraction in Key West is the 13,000 square foot Key West Butterfly and Nature Conservatory located at 1316 Duval Street. It is also Key West's newest attraction, having been completed in January 2003.

There are few attractions anywhere which appeal to young children, teenagers, their parents and grandparents. I have visited the conservatory four or five times, and have always been struck by the glee of the children and the wonderment in the eyes of the senior citizens. Virtually all visitors walk away from this butterfly world with a plastic butterfly attached to their shirt or sweater and a smile on their face.

The creators of this world of beauty are Sam Trophia and George Fernandez. They dreamed, planned and traveled the world to visit virtually every major conservatory. Their journey took them from Central, South, and North America, to Africa and Southeast Asia. Their aim was to build the best butterfly conservatory in the world. In addition to the 5,000 square foot glass-enclosed butterfly habitat are a learning center for children and a unique art gallery. There is also a beautifully decorated gift shop where it is extremely difficult to decide what to purchase because there are so many interesting, reasonably-priced choices available.

The partners' slogan is "Excite your senses, expand your mind." With over 60 varieties of butterflies, a few thousand plants, and at least 1,000 butterflies flying and landing on everything, that is exactly what happens. During one of my visits, two butterflies landed on my cap and stayed for a nice chat. . . The kids around me could not stop giggling and laughing at the sight!

CONCH TRAIN
Front Street

In 1959, Olive and Bill Kroll converted a dream into a money machine. With Olive selling tickets for $1.00 a ride, Bill would take the tourists on a ride, showing the prominent homes of Key West and other Key West attractions. In 1972, the large conglomerate, Wometco, purchased the Kroll's dream and in 1983 it was resold to Historic Tours of America.

The rides are open 365 days a year and utilize 14 trains (the cars are converted jeeps) which can comfortably accommodate 56 passengers. With inflation, the cost of today's ride has increased slightly to $20.00 per head. Over 11 million passengers have enjoyed the conch train ride over the past 44 years.

SOUTHERNMOST POINT
Ocean and Whitehead Street

There are more "Kodak moments" shot at the Southernmost Point of the United States than at any home, attraction, or sunset in Key West. Virtually every person visiting paradise finds his or her way to this fascinating spot. For at least 70 years, there has been a monument or sign designating this area and proclaiming "Cuba 90 Miles." The current monument dates to 1983.

For over 50 years, the Kee Clan, originally from China, has been selling conch shells to tourists who come to have their picture taken at the Southernmost Point. Originally "Yankee" and his brother "Chinaman" started the business. Yankee's son, Albert, carried on in his father's footsteps.

MALLORY SQUARE

Because of its daily sunset festivals, which begin two hours before sunset, Mallory Square is one of the most famous locations in Key West. In the mid–1800s, the Mallory docks, then a series of wooden decks, catered to the wrecking business. That industry pushed Key West into the limelight and helped it become the richest city per capita in the United States. In 1963, the old wooden planks were exchanged for a concrete base, and in 1990 the piers were revamped for cruise ship use.

Every night there is a gathering of thousands, mostly tourists, who come to watch the ever-changing performance of skilled entertainers, and mingle with fifty or so artisans selling their hand-crafted jewelry, photos, clothing and numerous other items. However, this is all a preamble, because once the setting sun begins to flirt with the horizon, all attention is galvanized toward the water and the setting sun's gentle surrender to the horizon.

FORT ZACHARY TAYLOR
Historic State Park and Public Beach

This beautiful 87 acre park, with attractively curved beaches, is a national landmark that has played a significant roll in Florida's early development. Construction on the fort began in 1845 and continued until 1866. The fort was never completed. The fort has a very strategic location overlooking the Atlantic Ocean, and Gulf of Mexico. In 1850, it was named after President Zachary Taylor, who had died earlier that year.

In 1861, when the Civil War began, Captain John Brannon and his men occupied the fort on behalf of the Union Army. President Lincoln had ordered a blockade of all Southern ports. Fort Taylor made Key West an effective port to operate because their cannons had a three-mile range. During the Civil War, 199 confederate ships were captured trying to run the blockade. The fort was also used in the Spanish-American War, and World War I and II. The fort currently has the largest collection of Civil War artifacts in America.

When Fort Taylor was opened as a state park, its 1,000-foot beach was a wonderful addition to the limited beaches in Key West. Although the beaches are lovely, I would suggest having some footwear when you go swimming at Fort Taylor because of the numerous rocks in the water. The West Side of the park is ideal for fishing. There are picnic tables, showers, and a concession stand.

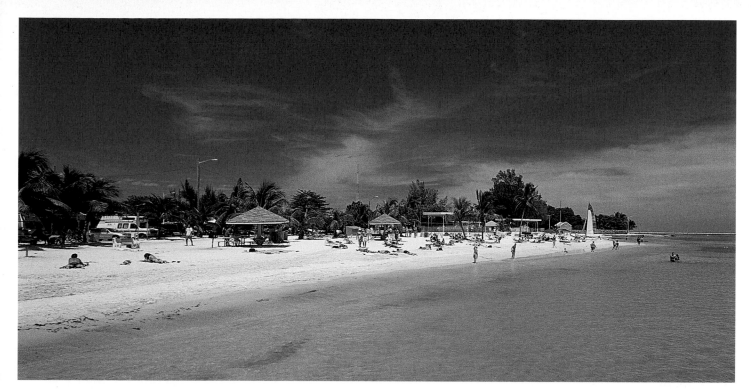

SMATHERS BEACH
South Roosevelt Boulevard

One mile from the Key West Airport, along the Atlantic Ocean, is Smathers Beach, named for Senator George Smathers. In 1961, the Senator was instrumental in getting federal funding, which helped create this beach. Smathers Beach runs for approximately one half mile in length, with numerous volleyball courts, rest facilities, and food vendors. This beach is a favorite with the tourists.

CLARENCE S. HIGGS MEMORIAL BEACH
South Roosevelt Boulevard

Higgs Beach was originally christened Monroe County Beach in April, 1949. Shortly thereafter, County Commissioner Higgs died and the name of the beach was changed in his honor. This manmade beach, jutting into the Atlantic slightly south of Smathers Beach, has a retaining wall, and a fascinating pier, with cleverly painted footsteps. The beach is adjacent to an old Civil War fort named West Martello Tower. Higgs Beach is a popular beach with the residents of Key West.

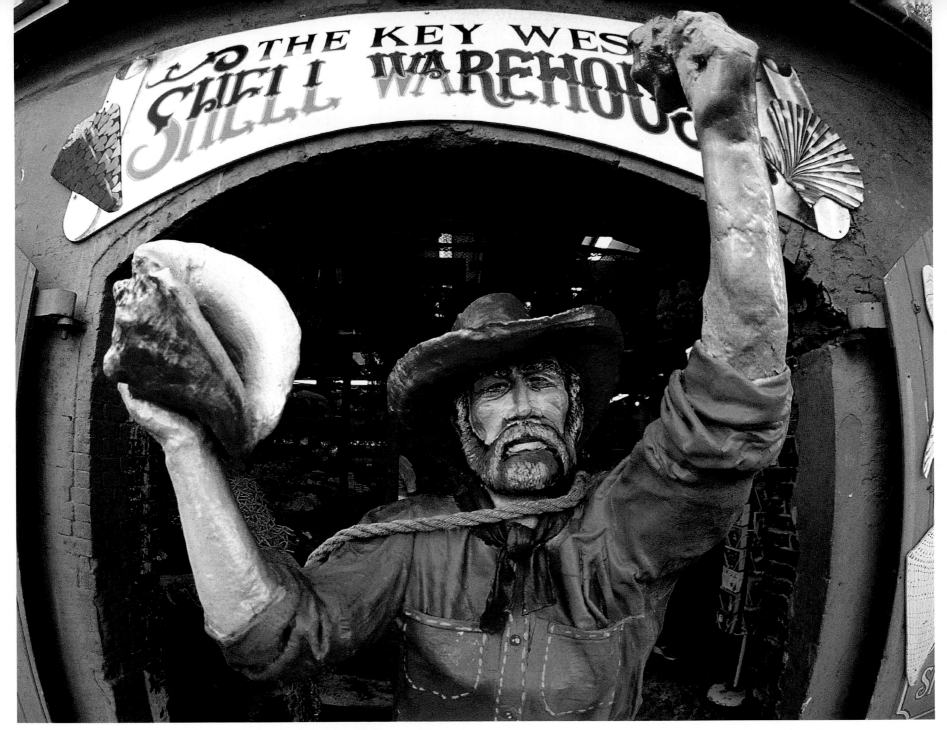

SHELL WAREHOUSE
1 Whitehead Street

If you love beachcombing and shell collecting as I do, the Shell Warehouse is a wonderful spot to enjoy and pick up a few small trinkets.

SUNSET KEY

In 1994, the property formally known as Tank Island was sold. This beautiful 27-acre property, a three-minute boat ride from Key West, has now been transformed into a tropical Island of elegance, beauty, and charm. The beaches are pristine and reminiscent of the silky, soft, white sands of the Caribbean. Millions of dollars have been invested into this unique vision. The natural beauty of this location combined with the creative and talented professional builders of Sunset Key has already attracted many families looking for their tropical paradise.

CRUISE LINES

The cruise ship industry is the fastest growing segment of the tourist trade in Key West. In 2003 approximately 1,000,000 passengers walked the planks into the golden sunshine of Key West. During the previous four years, that number had been under 700,000 travelers with small increases each year. In 1990, approximately 100,000 individuals disembarked in Key West to walk Duval Street for a number of hours, and in 1995 that had already increased to approximately 375,000 tourists, seeking a conch train ride or a beer at Sloppy Joe's.

Back in the mid-1970s, it was Carnival Cruise Line that pioneered the way with a new concept. The "Fun Cruise" was born, with flashy ships, great entertainment and gaudy casinos. This appealed to a mass market of young, first-time cruisers from all walks of life. The concept was brilliant! Today Carnival Corporation is the largest cruise ship company in the world, owning Carnival, Holland American, Cunard, Seabourn, Windstar and Costa Cruise Lines, with sales of approximately 4 billion dollars a year.

Opposite page-Carnival Glory

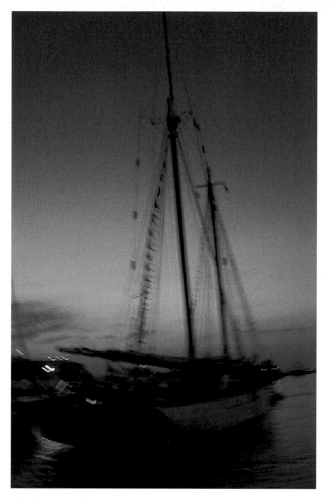

FLAT FISHING – DEEP-SEA FISHING

Tens of thousands of anglers come to Key West every year to fish. Dedicated golfers go to Scotland, and dedicated flat and sport fishermen come to paradise.

Norman Woods, Sr. is considered to be the father of Key West Marlin fishing. For many years it was well known that marlins were off the coast of Key West, as Hemingway proved in his years of fishing between Key West and Cuba. Beginning in the mid-1970s, Woods and his fishing buddy, Wayne Hunt, began searching for the escarpment, which drops 800 feet. The escarpment, or wall, runs parallel to the entire East Coast, and curves around the Keys and the Dry Tortugas and up into the Gulf of Mexico. This ridge creates an upwelling of nutrients on which baitfish feed. Larger fish feed on the baitfish, and the food chain continues as larger game fish feed on the other fish. One historic day in 1981 Woods found his paradise; he had seven marlins hooked and landed four of them. "We knew there had to be a drop off somewhere, and when we researched the charts we figured out where it had to be." The part of the escarpment of the lower keys is now known as "Woods' Wall," in honor of the pioneer who discovered it.

There are three members of the marlin family: the White Marlin, the Striped Marlin, and the big daddy, the Blue Marlin. They can range from 100 to 1,100 pounds and depending on the fish, the fisherman, the crew, and captain of the boat, the battle to catch the marlin can take from ten minutes to many hours.

FUN IN THE SUN

Before the sun sneaks away for a little nap and the serious partying begins, Key West is a camp for grown-ups with few restrictions and no counselors. There seems to be at least 15 varieties of automated transportation, including three-wheeled cars, electric cars, electric eggs, etc., which all seem to be carefree and fun, but certainly not inexpensive. Fishing, snorkeling, sailing, and scuba diving lure a high percentage of tourists. But don't forget wave running, kayaking, wind surfing, sunfish sailing, water skiing, speed boating, parasailing, jet skiing, roller blading, skateboarding, and that old time sport . . . swimming.

Opposite page: The beautiful catamaran, Stars & Stripes - Captained by Don Kincaid

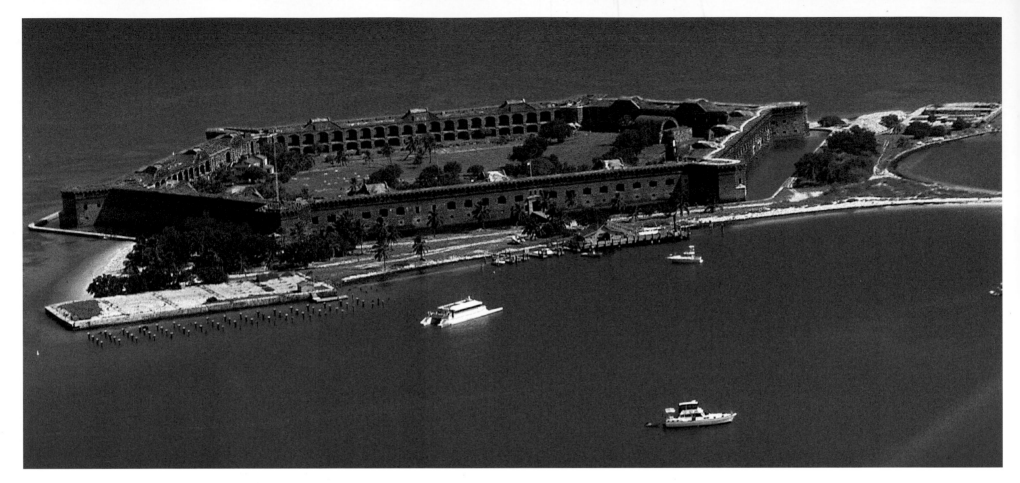

THE DRY TORTUGAS – FORT JEFFERSON

The most exciting adventure I experienced in Key West was a four-hour trip to the Dry Tortugas with Seaplanes of Key West. This national park lies in the blue-green waters of the Gulf of Mexico, 70 miles due west of Key West. The 40-minute plane ride is thrilling. Usually, the seaplane flies at an altitude of only 500 feet and the shallow waters enable you to see numerous shipwrecks lying in beautiful sparkling waters. If you are lucky, you may also get to see stingrays, porpoises, or sharks.

The Spanish explorer, Ponce De Leon discovered the islands in 1513. He named these seven small islands, La Tortugas (The Turtles), due to the abundance of sea turtles. The word "dry" was later added to mariners' charts to warn of the lack of fresh water. The first construction in 1825 on Garden Key, the largest of the seven islands, was a lighthouse to warn sailors of rocky shoals. Construction of Fort Jefferson began in 1846. The United States Military knew it could control the navigation to the Gulf of Mexico and protect Atlantic-bound trade by fortifying the Tortugas. For over 30 years, and utilizing over 16,000,000 bricks, construction continued on the 11 acres on Garden Key. However, the fort was never completed.

Continued on page 67

THE DRY TORTUGAS *continued*

During the Civil War, the fort was used by the north as a military prison for captured deserters. It also held Dr. Samuel Mudd, who was convicted of complicity in the assassination of President Lincoln in 1865. Because of the heroic work Dr. Mudd did during a yellow fever epidemic at the fort, which saved both soldiers and prisoners, he was pardoned, but not exonerated by President Jackson. Today a number of relatives of Dr. Mudd are still fighting in court to have him exonerated. However, there seems to be little doubt that he was involved in a conspiracy to kidnap Lincoln, lead by John Wilkes Booth, and therefore it is unlikely his relatives will be successful.

The invention of the rifled cannon made the fort obsolete because its thick walls could be penetrated. The army abandoned Fort Jefferson in 1874. In 1935 the fort was proclaimed a national monument, and in 1992, the Dry Tortugas reached its current status as a national park.

The Dry Tortugas are also a marine wilderness, and the main island is partially surrounded by beautiful beaches, which encourage snorkeling enthusiasts. Most of the individuals reach the island via catamarans and various schooners, which are housed in Key West.

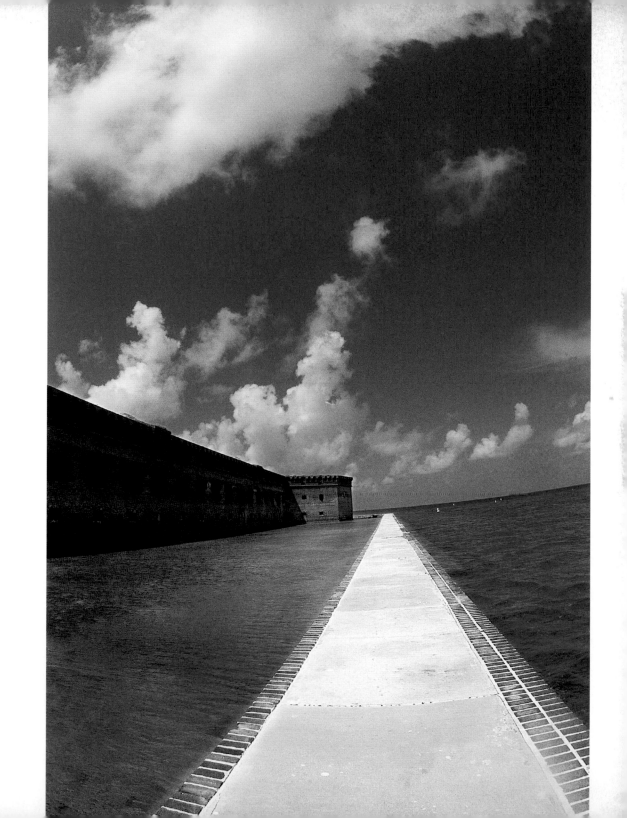

DUVAL STREET
Day

Duval Street begins at the Gulf of Mexico and runs for almost two miles with the Atlantic Ocean its final destination. Between these two beautiful bodies of water lie fourteen blocks of numerous restaurants, guesthouses, many excursion booths, hundreds of retail stores, and at least 436 T-shirt shops. During the day, these streets are the spokes of the wheel of Key West, as they teem with sightseers, shoppers, gays, straights, men, and women of all ages who have been lured by the hype of the southernmost city in the United States.

DUVAL STREET
Night

Key West comes alive at night, orchestrated by bars like Sloppy Joe's, Hog's Breath, Captain Tony's, and numerous others, which are directly on Duval or just a few steps away. Most bars have singers and bands to compete for the business of the tourists who have come to Key West to laugh, drink, and drink some more. At 1 a.m. most nights, there are generally more people walking the heart of Duval, than at 1 p.m., many with beer cans and bottles, and a little more boisterous than they were a few hours before. Duval at night is reminiscent of the French Quarter of New Orleans.

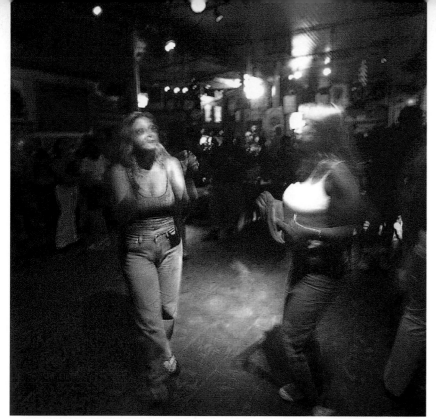

SLOPPY JOE'S
201 Duval Street

To me, Sloppy Joe's is the most famous bar in the world, with Rick's of Casablanca fame a close second. Back in the early 1930s, it was christened "Hemingway's Bar" by the Key West Chamber of Commerce. At that time, Sloppy Joe's was operating 24 hours a day; gin sold for 10 cents a shot, and a tall cool glass of beer, cost a nickle.

The original Sloppy Joe's, also world renowned, was located 90 miles southwest in Havana, Cuba. In 1928, when Hemingway first visited Key West, Joe Russell (Sloppy Joe), had already opened his gin mill, and was also captain of his own fishing boat. Joe Russell almost immediately became a key player in what was described as the Hemingway Mob, which included writer John Dos Passos.

Russell moved Sloppy Joe's three times. In mid-1937, at the expiration of his lease and after a disagreement with his landlord, he gave Key West something to talk about. At the stroke of midnight, he gathered all his drinking buddies together and literally ripped out the bar, the mirror, the fixtures, (including the urinals), and moved them to an empty location down the street. Joe paid off his moving men with free beers, and the drinking continued into the wee hours of the morning. Hemingway himself ended up with one of the urinals, which is currently on display in the garden of the Ernest Hemingway Home and Museum. In future years, Hemingway's comment concerning the Sloppy Joe's midnight move was, "Only in Key West."

THE CURRY MANSION INN
511 Caroline Street

William Curry was a penniless Bahamian when he first arrived in Key West in the 1820s. He later became the Treasurer of Key West, and was also credited with operating an unofficial bank for businesses and individuals. He is generally considered to be the first millionaire in Key West. Salvaging goods from the hapless ships which were engulfed by the coral reefs helped create his fortune. In the early years, many of the inhabitants of Key West considered the pirates and the scavengers of salvage as two peas in a pod.

Curry started building his mansion in 1867. Curry, like all wreckers who built homes in Key West, incorporated architectural details from many ports of call such as balustrades from New Orleans, columns from the deep South and the widow walks from New England. In 1905, the younger Curry constructed a new house on the original plot.

The 11,000 square foot house is furnished with 18th Century antiques and Victorian pieces, creating a charming and interesting throwback to a bygone era.

THE SOUTHERNMOST HOUSE
1400 Duval Street

This magnificent example of Queen Ann architecture is the shinning jewel of Key West. Judge J. Vinning Harris built this elegant structure in the early 1900s. Mrs. Harris, formerly Florida Curry, was the daughter of William Curry.

During the 1940s, this home was converted into a popular waterfront restaurant and gambling club, known as the Casa Cayo Hueso Club. It attracted many notables, such as Walter P. Chrysler and Tennessee Williams. The house became a private residence again after being purchased by Hilario and Placeres

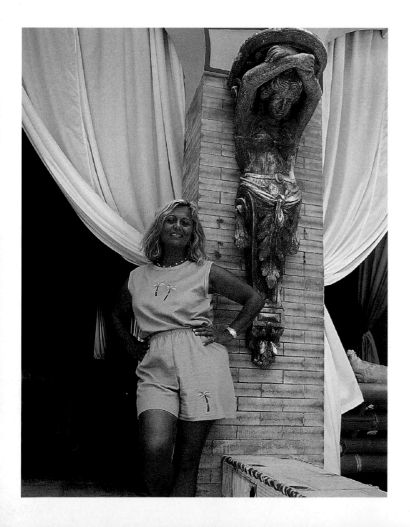

Ramos. Their children Charles and Mathilde, are the current owners. Charles Ramos has the distinction of being elected to the State Legislature in 1961 when he was only 24 years of age. Mr. Ramos also served as City Commissioner of Key West.

The Southernmost House has recently become a historic museum, with numerous, fascinating one-of-a-kind photos and documents of the history of Key West. This unique guest house, which is privileged by having it's own private beach, plays host to numerous romantic weddings using the Atlantic Ocean as a backdrop. There is also a beautiful outside bar area, surrounded by an inviting pool, which is attractively landscaped with potted plants and trees. This gorgeous oasis seems to have it all!

THE OCTAGON HOUSE
712 Eaton

The house at 712 Eaton has the unusual distinction of answering to three names. The Richard Peacon Jr. House, The Octagon House, and the Calvin Klein House.

Merchant Richard Peacon Jr., originally from the Bahamas, was the owner of Key West's largest grocery store. He completed 712 Eaton in 1899. Overflowing palms create a warm and inviting atmosphere surrounding this shimmering white house, adding to its romantic architectural lines. One of its nicknames, the Octagon House, is derived from its unusual facade, which is unique in Key West. Its elegance, both inside and out, has attracted two famous designers. In 1974, Angela Donghia purchased the house for $45,000 from Mrs. Chester Curry, the daughter of Richard Peacon. In 1980, after being renovated and restored by Fred Cole, the house was sold to Calvin Klein for $975,000, which up until that date was the highest price ever paid for a home in Key West. In less than a year, Klein lost his lust for Key West, and resold the house at a substantial loss. This only proves "Paradise" is not for everyone.

THE GINGERBREAD HOUSE
615 Elizabeth Street

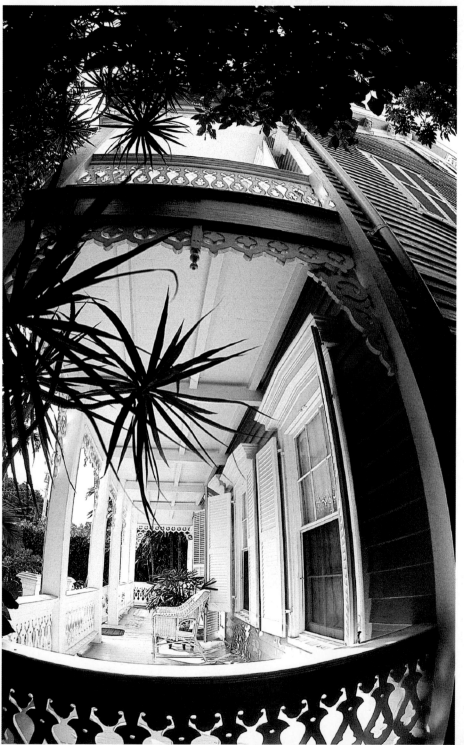

It is beautiful. . . It is unique. . . without a doubt, the best example of a large conch house with elaborate gingerbread details on the island. In 1870, Benjamin Baker, a Bahamian by birth, built the original structure, which over the years has undergone substantial renovation. Mr. Baker was a prominent citizen of Key West, serving as City Commissioner, as well as owning numerous businesses, which included undertaking, wrecking, sponging, and retail stores. Some of the old-timers of Key West, refer to this house as "The Wedding Cake House."

In 1885 the house was transferred to Mr. Baker's daughter when she married a gentlemen by the name of Illingsworth. The house stayed in the Baker-Illingsworth family for over 100 years, until it was sold in 1972. In 1995, this house was the recipient of the Preservation Award.

THE ERNEST HEMINGWAY HOUSE AND MUSEUM
907 Whitehead

The Man

The Hemingway myth is alive and flourishing in Key West. Even now, forty years after his death, the man who branded himself "Papa" while in his thirties, has continued to consume Key West and many of its tourists. The Hemingway saga, his writings, photos, articles and stories (including fabricated tall tales), live on in Key West through the Hemingway House, Sloppy Joe's, and numerous other retail establishments (who know that Hemingway paraphernalia sells. . . and sells big!).

Ernest and his second wife Pauline arrived in Key West in 1928. Hemingway was 28 years of age and a relatively unknown writer. When he left twelve years later in 1940, he had already published most of his important works and was world renowned for both his writing and the mystique which surrounded him.

The House

The Hemingway Estate is a one-acre, beautifully landscaped palatial home, guarded by a five-foot brick wall, which surrounds the property. Asa F. Tift, a successful merchant and shipbuilder originally built the house in 1851. Many conchs still refer to this house as the Asa Tift House. The house is constructed of limestone blocks from Key West, and was later remodeled. At the height of the depression in 1931, the Tift House was in deplorable condition and was in foreclosure. Gus Pfeiffer, Pauline's uncle, purchased the house from the bank for $8,000 and gave it to the Hemingways. A catwalk was built from the second level of Hemingway's writing studio to make it

continued next page

easier for him to go back and forth from the main house to his studio. In 1938, while Papa was covering the war in Spain, Pauline, in a futile attempt to save her marriage and to keep Hemingway away from the beautiful, bright, sexy writer, Martha Gellhorn, built a large swimming pool in their backyard. This was the very first pool in Key West. When he returned from Spain, in typical Hemingway fashion, he proclaimed to Pauline and to all his friends that the pool had cost him his last penny, as he tossed a penny on the ground and stated, "You might as well take my last cent." Pauline had that penny permanently fixed in cement at the edge of the pool where it remains today. It's interesting to note Pauline, not Hemingway, paid for the pool.

SIMONTON COURT HISTORIC INN & COTTAGES

320 Simonton Street

The combination of archways built with thousands of tiny magenta bougainvillea leaves, coupled with radiant flowers from orchid trees, create a setting in this garden that could lead to the Gates of Heaven. Strangely enough, the inn of this little paradise was a cigar factory in the 1870s, where tobacco leaves were dried, rolled and stored. Across from the inn is a series of small cottages, whose original tenants were the workers of the cigar factory. Today these cottages are surrounded by an impressive collection of palms, banana trees, ficus hedges, gardenia plants, orchids and bougainvillea which create an exotic atmosphere.

ST. PAUL'S EPISCOPAL CHURCH
401 Duval Street

Since 1832, St. Paul's has had a strong influence on Key West. In those days the real estate tax was set at "not more than one half of one percent," and unimproved land, which was almost the entire island, was valued at $25.00 per acre. In December 1832, John William Charles Fleming, who was one of the founding fathers of Key West, was buried on church ground. The church now stands on land given to St. Paul's by Mrs. J.W.C. Fleming for a consideration of $1.00.

The church has proved its resiliency by living through three major fires and three serious hurricanes. The church was destroyed on numerous occasions. The magnificent white masonry church currently on display with its beautiful stained-glass windows was built in 1919. The beautiful tree in full bloom in front of the church is a Royal Poinciana. It bursts into bloom just before the rainy season and blossoms like a flame. Its scarlet blooms are shed about two months later when the tree leafs out. The churchyard has a myriad of plants that grow in the tropics. The crotons, ixora and other plants from Africa add color to the landscape of the garden, which also houses numerous palms, West Indian mahoganies, and various other small plants and ferns.

In back of the church is a small cemetery. There are major plans to change the landscape with waterfalls, an altar, and additional new plants. Although the gardens are beautiful, the new plans seem very exciting.

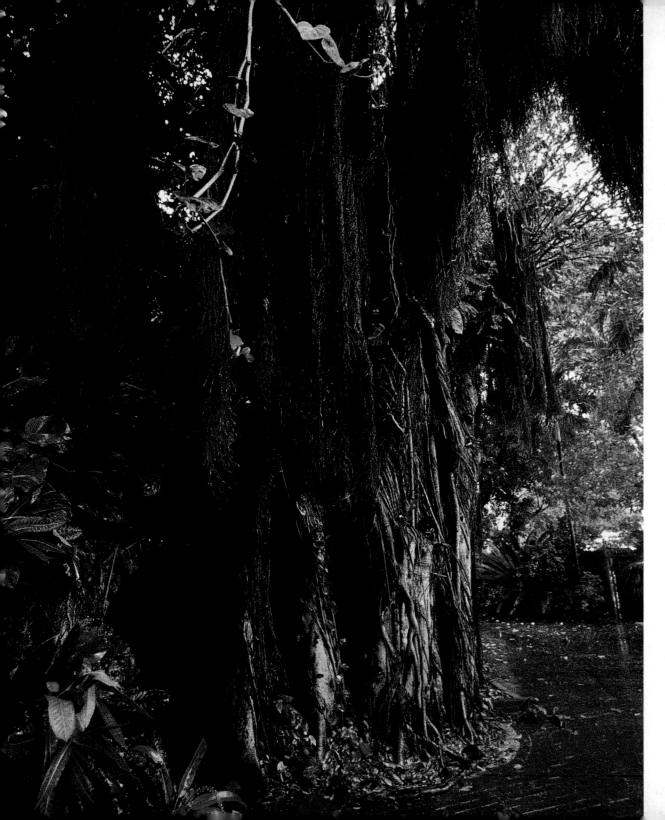

JOE ALLEN GARDEN CENTER
WEST MORTELLO TOWER
White Street at the Atlantic Ocean

I remember vividly my first visit to the Joe Allen Garden Center, which is cloistered in the West Mortello Tower. There was a major rainstorm and the huge drops felt like soggy pellets as they were attacking me. The plants and trees were glistening from the rain, appearing as if they had received three coats of shellac.

The West Mortello Tower is all that remains of a fort that was used in the Civil War. Years later, this fort was used for target practice for the large guns at Fort Taylor. Understandably, the entire remains were extremely unattractive and it was scheduled for demolition by the city of Key West. In 1949, a group of prisoners from the local jail arrived with sledgehammers to level the remains of the fort. Fate stepped in with the passing by of State Representative Joe Allen, who halted the destruction and shortly thereafter started to create a beautiful tropical garden, which became the Joe Allen Garden Center.

Since 1955, the Key West Garden Club has had the responsibility to care for, nurture, and enhance the Joe Allen Garden Center. There are 200 members of the garden club which meets once a month. Many of the members' personal gardens are the starting points for numerous plants before they are transplanted to the Joe Allen Garden Center.

NANCY FORRESTER'S SECRET GARDEN
Free School Lane

Discretely hidden off Simmonton, in the center of Old Town, is this unique acre of land consumed with trees, plants, and numerous parrots, which help create the feeling of a bygone era. When Charles Kuralt visited Nancy in her Secret Garden, he was thrilled to find her unusual collection of palms and flowers, which includes over a hundred varieties of palms from all over the world. This unusual collection has been brought together by Nancy and her many helpers for the past 30 years. One of her recent co-creators of the garden is Norman Aberle, an artist himself, and also the Curator of the Key West Museum of Art and History at the Custom House. After 20 years of creating a special habitat, Nancy opened her garden to the public in December 1994, with the following statement. "With every square inch of the island being covered with concrete, I needed to nurture myself with a garden, to stay in tune with the earth . . . I hope that people will come here and use it as a respite from the asphalt jungle. It's cool and tranquil and soothing here. It nourishes my spirit and soul."

Nancy's 17 parrots have begun to encroach on the time she can spend on the garden. Recently, when we met with Nancy, the general topic of conversation centered around her beautiful parrots. My associate took the time to teach Ara, a female macaw (opposite page), how to lift one of her wings. Nancy was very pleased with the new trick. Unfortunately, we didn't have enough time to spend with Dulce, a male Umbrella Cockatoo, who is pictured below.

The most unique and beautiful dining experience in a Key West vacation begins with a delightful (free) three-minute boat ride to the Island of Sunset Key. You will immediately be transported into a world of gentle breezes and elegant service, while dining on or near the beach, at the Lattitudes Restaurant. This romantic setting sets the mood for artistically-prepared delicious cuisine, while you await the sunset.

A few months ago while we were enjoying our dinner, we noticed a young, adorable couple sitting nearby. When the young lady excused herself, the young man leaned over and told us he was very nervous because he was going to propose after dinner, down at the dock. Fortunately, I had my camera and a short time later, although I was 300 yards away, I documented this romantic scene.